COUPLE SKILLS

How to Nurture Self-Love, Self-Appreciation and
Self-Respect. Cure and Transform Jealousy,
Insecurity and Attachment into Strengths for
Communication in Love and Couple Well-Being

By

Elliott J. Power

TABLE OF CONTENTS

CHAPTER 1
UNDERSTANDING THE IMPORTANCE
OF SELF-CARE

These days self-care is a common subject, but it's often poorly explained. Maybe you keep seeing it listed in self-help books or magazine articles, and yet you don't have a good sense of how to apply it to your life. You will find it wishy-washy or ambiguous. Alternatively, you might not be persuaded you should be doing routine self-care. Maybe you think that your money is saved better to work and to look after others.

So, what is self-care, and why does it matter so? There are, as it turns out, many different self-care habits, and not all of them suit everyone. This chapter will take you through the reasons in your routine why you need at least some form of self-care, and help you understand the practical changes you need to make.

What Is Self-Care? The Self-Care Concept

Self-care is a broad word that includes just about everything that you do for yourself to be healthy. To put it simply, it's about being as kind to yourself as you will be to anyone. It is partly about understanding when the resources run low, and stepping back to replenish them instead of making them all drain away.

In the meantime, it also includes incorporating self-compassion into your life in a manner that helps avoid even a burnout.

It is important to note, however, that not all that feels good is self-care. We can all be tempted to take advantage of unhealthy coping mechanisms such as drugs, alcohol, over-eating, and risk-taking. These self-destructive activities help us regulate emotional challenges, but the relief is temporary.

The difference between unhealthy mechanisms of coping and self-care is that the latter is uncontroversially good to you. When properly practiced, self-care has long-term benefits for the mind, body, or both.

Self-care advantages

With a definition of self-care on the table, we can turn now and look at what happens to us when we apply it to our lives. Why is self-care essential, then?

As indicated above, the benefits of self-care are many. The most evident relates to the levels of mood and electricity. The study, though, as it turns out, also shows broader benefits.

Top 6 Self-care benefits

- Improved rendering. When you learn to say "no" to things that exaggerate you and begin to make time for things that matter more, you slow down life in a wonderful way. This brings the goals to a sharper focus and lets you concentrate on what you're doing.

- Improved disease resistance; There is evidence that most practices of self-care trigger the Parasympathetic Nervous System (PNS). What this means is that the body enters a calming, rejuvenating state, helping it improve its immune system.

- Improved physical fitness. Similar to the previous argument, fewer colds, flu cases, and upset stomachs also come with improved self-care. Surely less tension and a stronger immune system will make you feel more physically healthy and strong inside and outside.

- Self-esteem improved. You send a constructive message to your subconscious when you consistently carve out time that is simply about being nice to yourself and fulfilling your own needs. Specifically, you have intrinsic worth and handle yourself like you matter. This can go a long way towards suppressing your critical inner voice and negative self-talk.

- Improved self-care. Practicing self-care allows you to think about what you want to do. The task of finding out what makes you feel inspired and motivated will help you understand yourself much better. This can also often spark a career change or a reprioritization of previously neglected hobbies.

- Contribute more. You may think you're egoistic when you're good to yourself. Self-care also gives you the support you need to be compassionate towards others. Giving compassion is a bit like filling a bucket; if you don't have enough of your own, you cannot fill anyone else's!

TYPES OF SELF-CARE

One of the principal reasons people make to neglect self-care activities is that they simply don't have time. The great news is that there are many different self-care activities, and none of them are overly daunting or require preparation. The trick is to find any you like and which suits your life and values. When you begin to incorporate emotional self-care into your life, you're likely to become intensely protective and wonder how you've ever been without it!

Here are the five major self-care categories, along with examples of how they can benefit you. We're also going to look at specific self-care examples within categories that should help you think about things you're going to enjoy, especially.

1. Sensory

Sensory self-care helps to help relax the mind.

When you are tuning in the specifics of the stimuli all around you, living in the present moment is simpler. And when you're in the moment, you can more easily let go of past-related resentments or potential anxieties.

Consider all the senses as you think about the practice of sensory self-care: touch, smell, sound, and sight.

Some people are more sensitive to one sense, so ask yourself what that meaning might be for you.

The following sensory self-care examples include at least one sense but sometimes more.

Sensory Suggestions for self-care

- Cuddling under a warm blanket.

- Driving out into the fields and reflecting on the air scent.

- Watching candle fires or a flare.

- During a hot bath or shower, feel the warmth on your face.

- The emphasis on your breathing patterns.

- Lying down with your eyes closed and listening to the album.

- Sitting at sunny afternoon temperatures.

- Have a square of the most delicious chocolate available.

- Walk barefoot across the grass.

- Massage using essential oils.

- Carry a pet in the arms.

2. Emotional

One of the best self-care tips when it comes to your mental wellbeing is to make sure you're completely involved with your emotions. In reality, this helps with tension when you face them head-on.

You may feel tempted to force down feelings like depression or rage but feeling them, acknowledging them, and moving on is safe.

Know the emotions in themselves are not "good" or "evil." You are not to blame for the emotions you feel;

you are to blame only for how you react to them.

Consider one or more of the following on this subject if you wish to practice better emotional self-care ...

Ideas about mental self-care

- Carry a regular publication and be completely frank about your thoughts.

- See a psychiatrist, even though this is only for 8-10 general personal growth sessions.

- Write a list of "things you know" to broaden your vocabulary.

- Make time to be with a friend or member of your family who knows you.

- Let's cry when you have to.

- Invite yourself to laugh with old memories or funny images.

- Sing along with a song that reflects the current feelings best.

3. Spiritual

If you are not religious, you might be tempted to

skim-read or miss this segment entirely.

Spiritual self-care, though, isn't just about believing in a god. It refers just as much to the atheists and agonists as to religious people.

Spiritual self-care is about coming into harmony with your beliefs and what matters to you.

Self-care tips for depression also emphasize that it is crucial to your healing to develop a sense of purpose. Below are some flexible examples that can help.

Ideas about personal self-care

- Continue the daily practice of meditation or mindfulness.

- Attend every service, religious or humanistic.

- Read some poems.

- Walk-in nature, and think of the beauty around you.

- Make a regular list of 5-10 items, which will make you feel thankful.

- Be imaginative, be it by painting, music, writing,

or something else.

- Make a list of 5-10 items that will make you feel good, then ask yourself how these items can be better integrated into your life.

- Say statements that underpin your sense of self and intent.

- Go on a trip with the sole intention of taking pictures of things that inspire you.

4. Physical

Indeed the value of self-care applies to strictly physical aspects of your wellbeing. Physical exercise is important not only for the well-being of the body but also to help you let off steam.

You may think there's nothing fun or self-compassionate about going to the gym, but that's just too limited a physical self-care way to think about. Instead, extend the concept by thinking about the lists below.

Ideas for Physical Self-Care

- Dance to the songs you love

- Yoga. Even if you have never tried it, the poses

are perfect for beginners.

- Attend a workshop and learn a new sport.

- Go running (or a friend's) with your puppy!

- Cycle down the countryside.

- Go only for a stroll.

Often note that physical self-care is about the stuff you don't do as much as the stuff you're doing! Thus:

1. Nap when the need arises. Just 20 minutes will make you feel comfortable mentally and physically.

2. Reply "no" to invites when you're just too lazy to have fun with them.

3. Do not force yourself to perform your workout routine when you are tired or are unwell.

4. Engage in 7-9 hours of nightly sleep, barring extraordinary circumstances.

5. Social

Lastly, social self-care is another category that is important to all of us.

Depending on whether you are an introvert or an

extrovert, it may look different. For a wide number of people, however, it is important to interact with other people for happiness.

It's making you realize you're not alone. Moreover, it can also give us a feeling of being truly "seen" by others. Particularly this can help us battle loneliness and isolation.

Social self-care isn't just about doing things for the benefit of others, but about wanting to do things for others that make you feel good.

Social Suggestions for self-care

- Arrange a lunch or dinner date with a wonderful friend.

- Send an email to someone who lives a long way away but loves you.

- Attain anyone you like but haven't seen them in a while.

- Consider joining a group of individuals who share your interests.

- Avoid socializing with the ones who discredit or

kill you.

- Strike up an engaging conversation with others.

- Join a support group for those dealing with the same problems as you do.

- Sign up for the class to learn more at the same time and meet new people.

TIPS ON SELF-CARE

1. Create a list of things that you are feeling restorative.

It might be taking a walk outside, petting your dog, meditating, baking, painting, arranging your wardrobe, listening to a podcast, or something else you enjoy calming tension.

"Save it on your tablet or anywhere you can easily access it," said Lauren Donelson, a Seattle writer and yoga instructor who is training to be a therapist. "Ideally, you'd make this list on a day that you're feeling pretty good, so that you don't have to worry about self-care things that you feel burned out — which happens to everybody."

2. Identify that for which you are thankful.

A lot is happening in the world, particularly right now, to be frustrated, angry, and scared about. But in these darker times, it is much more important to find things — large and small — that we're grateful for.

"We should turn our focus on what is positive in our lives on question our propensity to be drawn into negative thinking," said Tamara Levitt, head of mindfulness at the Peaceful meditation app. "Gratitude is a practice like everything else, and neuroscience teaches us that if we do our best to maintain love, we will find something to be thankful for, even in times of loss and sorrow."

Write down three items every day for which you are grateful in a newspaper, save them on your phone in the Notes app, or read them out loud with a loved one.

"It could be the health care staff or the service sector, the weather or a great piece of toast," "Your attempt to discover goodness in this chaos is a good exercise for your brain and mood."

3. Set Job limits.

With many people working from home, living spaces now act as office spaces and blur the distinction between work and play.

"It can be tempting to answer emails as soon as you wake up in the morning, or when you eat dinner, respond to messages from your boss," Donelson said.

Consider sticking to the same start and end times for your workday to build more structure.

"If you don't usually enter the office before 9 a.m., don't sign up for work before 9 a.m.," "And when you'd normally leave the workplace, stop working."

Place your laptop and any other work supplies in a cabinet, tub, or drawer while you're not on the clock until you need them again. Of sight, out of the heart.

4. Make a "done" list.

Taking a look at a long list of unfinished projects on your to-do list would just make you feel bad about yourself. Instead, I recommend making a "full" list of all of the things that you've already completed.

"Consider all of the things that you have accomplished, big and small, from grocery shopping to folding laundry to getting children through a school day," he said. "Beat yourself on the back to produce something at all at a time.

5. Put limitations on your absorption of news.

"Yeah, keeping up with the news and the latest trends is important, but not at the expense of your wellbeing, "When the news becomes a source of fear, anxiety, and futility, it's time to step back."

Block unique time slots to limit your consumption where you encourage yourself to read or watch the news and try to stop looking for updates otherwise.

"Respect the boundaries which you set and if you find that even a small dose of news feels too much, be aware of how you feel, and step away."

6. Open a book.

Put your mobile down and pick up a book.

"Take the book you intended to read and try to get 30 minutes of reading in a day. It just doesn't have to be 30 minutes straight. You might also break it up, three times a day doing something like 10 minutes reading.

7. Let yourself grieve the major and the minor losses.

People are currently grieving all sorts of losses: the loss of their loved ones, their careers, their health, their plans, their daily habits, just to name a few.

"What might feel like declining wellbeing with the crushing burden of your health care job or three children at home.

Take a breath and let yourself feel without judgment whatever you feel. I suggest when you're done, take a pen and paper and write down all the supporting forces in your life.

They may be "real, technical, economical, family-friendly." "The top-tier helpful colleagues, mentoring, the outstanding boss, the caring wedding vendors, the things you do, your strengths, or your ability to withstand tough times before and now."

8. Pause every day to check in on yourself.

Taking the time daily to check in with yourself will bring focus and understanding to a dizzying moment, otherwise. I suggest these three questions to ask yourself: "What's captivating your thoughts right now?

"; 'What feelings or physical sensations do you feel or experience? "And" What would you like to achieve today?

9. Try breathing exercises.

One of the favorite soothing practices is called "box breathing." The technique outlined below is popular among Navy SEALs, and takes only five minutes:

- Step 1: 4 seconds to inhale.

- Step 2: 4 seconds to hold air in your lungs.

- Move 3: Exhale for 4 seconds and clear all the air in your lungs.

- Step 4: Stay your lungs empty for 4 seconds.

- Step 5: Repeat 5 minutes.

10. Physical Care

Certainly, the value of self-care applies to solely physical aspects of your wellbeing. Physical exercise is important not only for the well-being of your body, but also for helping you to release steam.

You may think there's nothing fun or self-compassionate about going to the gym, but that's just too limited a physical self-care way to think about. Alternatively, extend the notion by thinking of the following lists.

Ideas for Physical Self-Care

- Dance to a favorite of your songs

- Do some yoga. Even if you have never done it, the poses are ideal for beginners.

- Undertake a workshop and try a new sport.

- Go run with your (or a friend's) puppy!

- Through the countryside, cycle.

- Simply go for a stroll.

Often note that physical self-care is about the stuff you don't do as much as the stuff you're doing! So:-So:

- Nap when it's important for you. Just 20 minutes will make you feel comfortable mentally and physically.

- When you're actually too exhausted to enjoy them, say 'no' to invitations.

- Do not force yourself to perform your workout

routine when you run down or are unwell.

- Engage in 7-9 hours of nightly sleep, barring extraordinary circumstances. 11. Creating a bedtime routine to foster healthy sleeping habits.

- Having a good night's sleep will set an optimistic tone for your day and help you manage your anxiety and stress better. Create a nighttime routine to encourage this that helps your body wind down and puts you in sleep mode.

Try to have a hot bath or shower because hot water will help lower the core body temperature required to start and sustain a good night's sleep," The Sleepy time tea and a decent book − and no scrolling Instagram! − And you're going to be out in no time.

12. Keep a journal.

If you feel weighed down by rushing thoughts, consider beginning a journaling practice. Setting aside some time to focus on yourself will help to relax your busy mind and to explain and process what you are feeling.

"If it's something you're dealing with, try to take 10

minutes a day to focus on how you feel, write down any worries or doubts, and agree it feeling these things is Normal.

Not sure where to get started? Some journaling exercises can be found online or in books that contain prompts and questions designed to sharpen your introspection skills.

"Daily self-reflection helps you remain linked to yourself, which means that when external elements in your life start to change, you can retain your inner balance and power.

13. Be extra gentle.

These days, are they not shooting on all the cylinders? Take the slack on yourself. Many people find it hard to feel less inspired than normal when they really should practice self-compassion.

"Instead of beating yourself up for not being 'leveling-up' right now, consider validating yourself with good self-talking," she said. "Like, 'This is hard.' 'My body reacts to an immediate threat.' 'I am not alone'"

Consider what you would say during this time to a

dear friend or relative who is struggling. "Then say these things to yourself."

40 MORE THOUGHTS ON SELF-CARE

1. Practice replacing the words with the 'should.'

2. Take another path to work or the stores.

3. Catch an episode from your favorite television show. Write down than five reasons why you like it.

4. Build a modern, safe, day-to-day routine, and incorporate it into your life.

5. Ignore spammy emails.

6. Reflect on past successes and milestones.

7. Take 15 minutes to drink the heat.

8. Please visit the nearest library.

9. Do a job in your home that you have put off.

10. Watch videos and speeches which are motivating.

11. Speak to a loved one about their own thoughts or habits about self-care.

12. Let's joke!

13. Write a summary of a business you have recently

enjoyed (such as a restaurant or product you've bought).

14. Create your room.

15. Work on a puzzle you like, a Sudoku puzzle, crossword, or jigsaw, for example.

16. Start a journal.

17. Write out a new statement.

18. Make sure you currently drink at least eight glasses of water.

19. Dance like nobody watches.

20. Learn how to do a massage to yourself.

21. Write a message to the older self.

22. Write a letter to the old self.

23. Do a Digital Detox for 6 hours.

24. Go to your theater.

25. Do something to benefit charity.

26. Clean your car, handbag, and jacket pockets, if necessary.

27. Find a local counselor or therapist.

28. Do something fun that you used to do as a child.

29. Cook a meal you never had before.

30. Do local history research.

31. Set up regular phone notifications to remind you that you're great!

32. Clean your desk or place of employment.

33. Watch a documentary.

34. Take a day of mental health when you feel especially depressed and call in sick to work.

35. Change your bedsheets and have a night early.

36. Read your favorite book over again.

37. Consider forming a community group in your local area.

38. Read motivational quotes.

39. Create a self-care box filled with items like candles, essential oils, affirmation cards, ideas about self-care, a book, etc.

40. Smile in the mirror!

CHAPTER 2
OVERCOMING ATTACHMENT ISSUES

When it comes to the state of their interpersonal relationships or other relationships in general, nervous individuals will be well-served to accept ways of resolving attachment problems as a major step towards enhancing the social aspects of life.

A clinician will help them to understand their internal models of practice, how they relate to others, their early experiences, and their relationships with other people. The adjustment of their working models to reflect the complexities of new experiences and relationships may be a significant goal in therapy.

UNDERSTANDING VARIOUS ATTACHMENT STYLES

Attachment Classification

Researchers Bowlby, Harlow, and Lorenz demonstrate through their Evolutionary Theory of Attachment that children bind themselves predominantly to one individual during early infancy and childhood (ages 0-5). Typically it's the mother (or replacement mother), and this relationship is a blueprint for all future relationships.

If the relationship between parent and child ends, is broken, or otherwise is dysfunctional, it can have a detrimental effect on future ties. It is these encounters (or lack of them) that lead humans to form one of the following three types of attachment

1. Stable mounting type

While Hollywood and current popular culture can categorize secure attachment as "boring" or "mundane," it is from this style of attachment that solid, healthy ties are born. A stable attachment ensures that every person in the relationship feels safe, looks after, and understands. Kids who are firmly attached also develop into strong, healthy adults.

The variations in attachment styles and how they affect our lives are becoming ever more evident when assessing the success and happiness rating of securely attached children versus unsafely attached or avoiding forms.

Interestingly, this is not perfect parenting or even a lack of parenting skills, which determines the style of attachment. When a caretaker can make a child feel safe and secured via nonverbal communication, stable attachment grows. Factors which prevent attachment protection from forming include:

- Abuse or maltreatment

- The only concern when doing poorly or behaving badly

- Occasionally or inconsistently, getting your needs addressed

- Separation from parents (e.g., hospitalization, a departure from home)

Children who are tightly attached to their parents during their infancy:

- They choose to be with his/her parents over others.

- They should isolate themselves from their parents without being too angry.

- If they're scared, look for support from their parents.

- They are happy when they return to see their friends.

Similarly, people who have been securely attached as children to their parents appear to have long-term relationships in which they trust their partners and display a high level of self-esteem. Not only are these folks comfortable sharing with their partners their thoughts, hopes, and dreams, but they can also seek support when needed.

Stable people are also able to support and console their friends when they're suffering. Individuals with a stable style of attachment appear to become great partners.

2. Anxious-preoccupied form of attachment

If you can't relate to the first form of attachment when it comes to explaining discrepancies in attachment types, you possibly developed an insecure style of attachment during childhood or the fourth style of attachment, which is nervous.

There is an anxious attachment style among about 15 to 20 percent of people. Many people in this state of mind are seeking therapy because of the difficulties they face when trying to develop stable adult attachments.

Many stressed carers are distracted or otherwise unable to consistently meet the needs of their children. People who form this kind of connection were not abandoned as children, and in most cases, their parents showed some care and concern for them; however, they did not fully establish their inner feelings of security as children. The inconsistent treatment has meant that they cannot rely on their parent or another caregiver.

This incoherence creates an emotional storm inside the anxious child, which translates into adulthood and can contribute to relationship-avoiding types of people.

Like those individuals with a stable attachment style, people with the attachment style of an insecure child desire affection and intimacy but also experience a lack of self-worth. This negative self-esteem is directly linked to their attachment protection to their attachment figure.

Attachment types in early childhood maintain themselves, the attachment theory says. Their deep-rooted insecurities can lead to behaviors that seek attention (or antisocial actions for types that avoid it). While many good people are caring, friendly, all-around, their clinginess, neediness, envy, and ability to nag many drives loved ones away.

Popular characteristics of the type of relationship an anxious child has included:

- A need for reassurance from friends and consistent affirmation.

- A desire from partners or potential partners for continuous contact, interaction, and focus.

- Serious High and Low Partnerships.

- A sensation of distress or fear when separated (even temporarily) from a partner.

- A propensity to use blame, guilt, shame, and other types of coercion to hold the partners close.

- A propensity to ignore duties because of an interest in relationships or personal interests.

- A propensity to overreact when the partnership is considered to be under pressure. These risks could, in some cases, be imagined.

If the above characteristics reflect your habits, obviously you are not alone. While an insecure attachment style can make building and maintaining stable long-term relationships challenging, it is important to remember that styles of attachment are complex and can be changed with understanding, self-acceptance, and function.

3. Removable attachment

A sort of dismissive-avoiding attachment is the polar opposite of the type of attachment that is anxiously worried out above. Though the two types have one similarity — both are vulnerable — these styles of attachment couldn't be any different. Emotionally detached and avoiding, people with a sort of dismissive relationship don't desire love; in reality, they run away from it.

Interestingly, several forms of nervous attachments are associated with dismissive-avoidant partners in relationships and marriages. The more the insecure partner strives for love and approval, the further it separates him or herself from the insensitive partner. The non-evitable partner, upset by this lack of intimacy, will threaten to end the relationship, which will have little impact on the dismissive partner.

Capable of detaching themselves from others, shutting down completely, and living their lives inwardly, folks with a dismissive style of attachment give off a pseudo-independence that implies that they need no relation. That is, of course, simply untrue.

You have noticed a pattern by now. The avoidance of intimate relationships is the consequence of childhood events in which a caregiver was unable or unable to build a secure connection to the parent.

Parents were physically present in some cases, but for one reason or another, they were unable to fulfill the emotional needs of their children. In this situation, the child learns to suppress the feelings and repress them. When looking at contrasting variations in attachment styles — securely attached kids usually show a higher level of satisfaction with their adult lives than precariously attached kids.

This dysfunctional attachment style for avoiding forms brings adulthood, and the grown person avoids the need for love and connection. Typically the following characteristics occur when a person has a form of avoiding attachment:

- Intense emotions and personal circumstances make them anxious

- They set emotional and/or physical limits to extremes

- It can conceal information from its partners

- They send out mixed messages and ignore the feelings of partners

- They are selfless and enjoy casual sex

- Past partnerships are idealized

While avoidant types may have a deep desire for close relationships and intimacy, due to their deep-seated internal challenges, they are usually unable to satisfy their desires. Avoidant forms are more likely to indulge in sexual affairs and divorce themselves.

According to attachment theory psychology, people with an avoiding attachment style need to transition to a stable attachment style to form and sustain healthy relationships. Like any form of attachment, this change is possible if directed by a mental health professional who understands the attachment process.

A licensed therapist will work with your primary relationship figure — and yourself to address unresolved problems. Adults and children who are safely attached experience considerably less pain in their lives.

If you want to learn more about how your relationship with your primary attachment figure has changed your life, speak to a licensed therapist specialist focused on attachment theory and attachment technique, who is trained in counseling.

Since it's challenging for avoidant types to express their emotions, seeking counseling can be a daunting process. Still, it's a vital and essential step to help them move towards stable attachment.

4. Disorganized form of attachment

The final form of attachment is not based solely on frustration or anxiety but on extreme fear as well. The attachment figure of children with a disorganized form of attachment typically manages the trauma themselves. The attachment figure is unable to bind itself firmly to the child because of unresolved trauma, pain, or loss. Eighty percent of those exploited as a child have this kind of attachment.

Since the actions of their primary attachment figure were always unpredictable and fear-driven, adults with that kind of attachment style have never learned to soothe themselves. Their history is marked by pain and loss, and they may become violent, look upon the world as dangerous, and otherwise have psychological problems. Signs of that type of attachment include:

- A hot/cold mentality concerning relationships.

- Antisocial conduct and inadequate remorse.

- A tendency towards selfishness, self-control, and lack of personal responsibility.

- The recreating of dysfunctional behaviors in

adult relationships from their youth.

- Drug and alcohol misuse and criminal acts of violence or devastation.

If you think you may have some sort of disorganized attachment, don't be discouraged. With the aid of a licensed counseling specialist, you will learn how to become safely attached. Information is crucial once again. Education, motivation, and counseling will help you move towards a stable style of relationship, so you can develop good, healthy ties.

Additional Resources

The ambivalent type of attachment is debated less regularly. It's akin to the nervous attachment. When a carer is seen as unreliable, ambivalent attachments form, it may be they are disinterested in the development of the infant, or they are interested but not always present. Whatever causes attachment formation, adults with an ambivalent attachment pattern can show a lack of attachment in adult relations. They may be disinterested in forming new relationships, but they may experience love development, sensitivity, and attachment to individuals with whom they spend a great deal of time.

The protection of attachment in infancy may result in adult persons being securely attached. However, as with the outcomes of adult relationships, the role of attachment can shift, as can the types of sensitivity and attachment.

For example, avoiding attachment styles appear to evolve in adults who may have had stable attachments in childhood and then experienced problematic relationships.

You've heard in this book that counseling can be life-changing for people with non-secure forms of attachment. Online therapy provides a comfortable place to address your problems, and best of all, you can enjoy the benefits without leaving your home comfort.

What does Attachment Patterns mean?

Attachment patterns demonstrate that people as adults develop relationship styles based on attachment patterns from early childhood. In the pre-school years, we are told to start practicing learned attachment when we start communicating with others outside our family. According to the attachment theory, in early infancy and childhood, our main attachment styles secure themselves in place.

When it comes to the various forms of attachment and the roots of attachment theory, people with children who are securely attached usually see these children develop into adults who are firmly attached to them. As a result, people with stable relationship styles will possibly feel more positive in themselves and their surroundings. The theory of attachment works based on the assumption that securely attached infants (and securely attached children) become secure adults.

Safe forms have an air of trust and certainty, which seems to lack in the other styles of attachment. People with unsurely attached styles are less self-confident and distrustful of their world. It is assumed that firmly attached infants do better than adults. The mental health professionals, such as psychologists and therapists' main attachment approach are to help people who formed unstable attachments in early childhood, learn how to develop more stable attachments.

How are attachment forms evolving?

The attachment patterns and attachment types are formed in early childhood according to attachment research and attachment theory. The theory of attachment works under the assumption that children securely attached to it can develop to become adults securely attached. The attachment model used in attachment theory research is focused on attachment style and relationship research being carried out using a mother, a stranger, and a child.

Could you change your type of attachment in adulthood?

Experts in psychology say people who are firmly connected tend to do better in life. But not everyone in early childhood was able to firmly connect themselves to their primary attachment figure. The good news is that in early childhood, adolescents who formed an unstable relationship with their primary attachment figure have opportunities for improvement.

Attachment theory teaches us it's possible to alter one's type of attachment in adulthood. By seeking professional support from a licensed therapist, you can learn how to alter unhealthy attachment behaviors and build a healthy attachment style. A therapist will help you learn about the origins of the philosophy of attachment and the four ways of attachment.

These four types of attachment (created by our interactions with our primary figure of attachment) set the stage for how our emotional connection and relationship ties will develop over time. Conversing with a mental health professional will help you explore how the forms of attachment impact your life. In counseling, you will discover how childhood trauma still affects you today. You and your therapist will work together to develop an attachment plan that can help you develop a healthy attachment style — considering your past attachment behaviors.

It's possible to change your attachment styles once you start to understand the differences in attachment styles and attachment protection. Adult attachment styles like anxious-evitating attachment, avoiding attachment forms, and unstable attachment styles can be modified using a personalized attachment approach based on the principles used in attachment theory.

Unfortunately, both ways swing the door-so as to speak. Children who have formed stable attachments may develop other types of attachment, such as rejecting attachment styles, if they have challenging experiences in relationships later in life without the support networks to function healthily through their emotions and experiences.

What are the examples of behaviors about attachment?

Securely attached infants have a preference for their attachment figure when it comes to attachment protection and the prime attachment figure. Safe forms display earlier flexibility and greater self-confidence when exploring their surroundings. In comparison, insecurely attached children are less confident in their actions when interacting with others and their environment, and less and more negative.

The variations in attachment types are reflected in the variations in the study of children's self-confidence levels and behaviors. Anxious-avoidant attached infants are oblivious to their attachment figure, or a stranger, being present.

The attachment figure can display disdain or disinterest in insecurely attached infants. Because of this detrimental experience of infant attachment, these habits are likely to pass into infancy and eventually adulthood. If you have trouble with a dysfunctional child attachment-related relationship, talking to a licensed counseling professional will help.

What is an illustration of the attachment?

An attachment figure is an early caregiver that serves as the basis for an attachment to a child. Attachment statistics are known to have a lasting impact on our lives. In attachment research, contact with the attachment figure focuses primarily on the mother's attachment to the child. However, if there was no mother present (or if the mother was not the primary attachment figure), attachment theory and attachment patterns of the infant are looked at about the caregiver present.

Attachment figures are thought to play a significant role in whether or not children develop secure attachments. Attachment styles of a child are developed in response to the affection and care the attachment figure gives. The attachment figure gained more affection, support, attention, and care from people with stable attachment styles than avoiding forms of unstable forms of attachment styles.

A child needs to feel comfortable and secured to build a stable relationship with the primary attachment figure. Attachment types are shaped about the mother or other attachment figure, based on the sense of protection and security the child feels.

What would you behave like in a relationship?

In their adult relationships, this person may be a bit insecure, "They might be insecure, very dependent, concerned about [a partner] going out with friends or having different interests. Unfortunately, what happens is that they cause arguments over these things in relationships. In extreme situations, they might end up being quite controlling, possessive and jealous. They might start doing a lot of check-ups, also covert surveillance like placing cameras in [a partner's] car.

"This is someone who displays no kind of jealous or possessive behaviour,"that's the couple where they don't do anything together, they have their own interests, they go out with friends as well as each other, they aren't jealous of each other, they aren't possessive, they don't keep checking in with each other, they don't have to keep calling or phoning to see where the other is.

What makes the attachment look insecure?

Depending on the type, an unstable adult attachment can look similar to a precarious infant attachment. For example, if an adult is affected by ambivalent attachment, the majority of the time, they may be nervous. They can also be seen as in a relationship involving a lot of emotional support. In a relationship, that could make people feel insecure.

What are the symptoms of Adult Attachment Disorder?

Signs of adult attachment disorder include influence, frustration, urges, and confidence issues. Also, people feel like they don't belong, can't be affectionate, and have difficulty in all kinds of relationships. The theory and research on the topic suggest that, regardless of age, treatment is needed to move beyond this kind of condition.

What Are the Attachment Disorder Symptoms?

Attachment disorder symptoms are similar to signs of attachment disorder. Other signs include aversion to people who love them, withdrawal from circumstances, and feeling hollow.

Do avoidant partners cheat?

An evasive partner could likely cheat. This means that if someone shows an avoiding adult attachment style, they may lie, which could be used as a coping strategy to prevent themselves from getting hurt or other people being close to them emotionally. Attachment theory and research have explored all forms of adult attachment to see how people act like adults when they have not received treatment formed as children for potential attachment problems. This is how they know how evasive partners will respond to certain romantic relationships between adults.

How do I know when I have problems with the attachment?

You may be able to tell if you have signs of a reactive attachment disorder that you have attachment issues. Some signs include having anger problems, manipulating, not trusting, not feeling you belong, or avoiding contact with others. If you have any of those symptoms, especially when it comes to romantic relationships, you can have problems with attachment. You should learn more about social psychology and adult attachment when you believe you have attachment problems that were a result of your childhood. You will then be able to decide for yourself whether you need to reach out to a therapist for assistance. This can translate into insecure attachment in adults, particularly if largely overlooked if a child does not develop a secure attachment with their caregivers.

How do you break an attachment?

Generally speaking, if you want to sever somebody's bond, you'll need to focus on it. To do so, you may also need a support system and counseling. If you're trying to break an unstable childhood connection, this might include clinical applications to assist you in the process.

Ways to resolve attachments issues in insecure relationship

If you think you are uncertainly attached and it has a detrimental effect on your love life, here are a few steps you may take to make the transition to stable attachment:

Get to know the pattern of attachment by reading up the theory of attachment. Trust me: Information is authority.

If you don't have a great therapist now with the experience in attachment theory, find one. It could also be worth asking if they've ever had a patient or client in their adult romantic relationships that they've seen make the transition from vulnerable to stable attachment.

Find for partners that have stable types of attachment. If you are trying to overhaul your attachment style, the last thing you need is to be undermined by someone who can't help you. Research shows that in their attachment style, about 50 percent of adults are secure-pretty good chances of finding someone out there who rocks the world AND is secure. Studies say that a positive encounter with a person who is certainly attached will overcome your insecure instincts in time.

If you haven't met a partner like this, go to couple therapy. If you are, say, anxious-concerned and you are already in a loving relationship with, say, someone who is fearful-avoiding, I would encourage you to find a couple therapist who can motivate both of you to become safer together. Even if you feel your relationship is going well, consider taking this measure as a pre-emptive strike to solve trouble.

Exercise. Isn't pillow talk just your thing? Do it yourself, even though you have to start talking to an animal that is stuffed up. Hate asking about your relationship's future? Try worrying about your relationship's next few months if you can't deal with worrying about the next few years.

It is also important to bear in mind that stable connection in intimate relationships not only makes such relationships more fulfilling; there is proof that it can connect with even such with whom you are not near.

48

Research suggests that "boosting" one 's protection in some way ("safety priming" in psychology circles) makes people overall more generous and compassionate. This study by leading attachment researchers indicates that "whether formed in a person's long-term relationship background or nudged up by subliminal or supraliminal priming, the sense of attachment security makes altruistic caregiving more probable."

My impression is that it's just like riding a bike for those trying to upgrade their attachment style from vulnerable to stable, as the saying goes: Once you've got it, you've got it. You can always push yourself over time to become a "better biker"—a stronger one, a quicker one, a more agile one — but once you've mastered looking forward and pedaling at the same time, you're still good to go.

CHAPTER 3
THE BENEFITS OF MEDITATION

For thousands of years, meditation has been practiced. Originally meditation was intended to help deepen awareness of the sacred and spiritual powers of creation. Meditation is widely used nowadays for relaxation and reduction of stress.

Meditation is used as a form of complementary therapy for the mind-body. Meditation will yield a deep state of relaxation and a relaxed mind.

You concentrate your attention during meditation, removing the stream of jumbled thoughts that can clutter your mind and trigger stress. This process will contribute to better physical and emotional health.

Advantages of meditation

Meditation will give you a sense of relaxation, peace, and stability, which will help both your mental well-being and physical health.

And those benefits don't end when your session of meditation is finished. Meditation can help to get you through the day more calmly and can help you control the effects of certain medical conditions.

Emotional health and meditation

When you meditate, you can clear off the abundance of knowledge that builds up every day and contributes to your stress.

Meditation can have the emotional benefits of including:

- Gaining new perspectives on difficult conditions

- Competencies building to handle the tension

- Improving self-confidence

- Focusing the present

- Reducing negative feelings

- Building up imagination and innovation

- Heightened awareness and endurance

Meditation and illness

Meditation can also be helpful if you have a medical problem, in particular one that can be exacerbated by stress.

Although a growing variety of clinical evidence supports meditation's health benefits, some researchers feel it is not yet possible to conclude the potential benefits of meditation.

With that in mind, some research indicates meditation can help people control disease symptoms such as:

- Anxiety

- Asthma

- Cancer

- Chronic pain

- Depression

- Heart disease

- High blood pressure

- Irritable bowel syndrome

- Problems with sleep

- Headache pain

If you have any of these disorders or other health issues, be sure to speak to your health care professional about the pros and cons of using meditation. In certain cases, meditation can exacerbate the symptoms associated with some conditions of mental and physical health.

Meditation is not a substitute for conventional medicine. But it can be a helpful supplement to the other medication.

Meditation Forms

Meditation is a paragliding term with several forms for a peaceful state of being. There are many kinds of meditation and relaxation techniques which have components of meditation. All hold the same aim of having inner peace.

Might include ways to meditate:

- Meditation recommended. Often called guided imagery or imagination, you create mental images of locations or situations you find soothing with this type of meditation. You are trying to use as many senses as you can, including smells, sights, sounds, and textures. A guide or instructor may guide you through that method.

- Meditation mantra. In this form of meditation, to avoid distracting thoughts, you quietly repeat a soothing expression, feeling, or phrase.

- Mindfulness meditation. This kind of meditation is focused on being vigilant or getting an increased understanding and appreciation of living at this moment. In meditation on mindfulness, you stretch your conscious consciousness. You reflect on what you feel during meditation, like your breath flowing. You should observe your thoughts and feelings but without judgment, let them pass.

- Qi gong. In general, this method incorporates meditation, relaxation, physical activity, and respiratory exercises to preserve and maintain equilibrium. Qi gong (CHEE-gung) is a part of Chinese traditional medicine.

- Tai chi. This is a gentle style of Chinese martial arts. In tai chi (TIE-CHEE), as you practice deep breathing, you execute a self-paced sequence of postures or moves in a steady, graceful manner.

- Transcendental   Meditation. Transcendental meditation is a simple technique which is normal. In Transcendental Meditation, in a particular way, you quietly repeat a personally defined rhythm, like a script, sound, or expression.

- This form of meditation can allow your body to settle into a state of deep relaxation, and your mind to attain a state of inner peace without the need for concentration or effort.

- Yoga. To foster a more relaxed body and a peaceful mind, you perform a series of postures and synchronized breathing exercises. You're encouraged to concentrate less on your busy day and more on the moment as you step through poses that need balance and concentration.

MEDITATION ELEMENTS

Various forms of meditation can include various features to help you meditate. This will differ depending on whose instructions you are following or who is teaching a lesson. In meditation, some of the most common features include:

- Focused attention. Generally, one of the essential aspects of meditation is to concentrate your mind.

- Focusing your focus is what helps release your mind from the multitude of distractions that trigger tension and worry. You may concentrate your attention on things like a particular object, an image, a mantra, or even a breath.

- Relaxed breathing. This technique involves fast, even-paced respiration using the muscle of the diaphragm to expand the lungs. The intention is to slow down your breathing, take in more oxygen, and reduce the use of the muscles of the shoulder, neck, and upper chest when breathing so that you breathe more effectively.

- A quiet setting. If you're a novice, it could be easier to practice meditation if you're in a quiet spot with few distractions, including no television, radios, or cell phones. You may be able to do it anywhere as you become more experienced in meditation, particularly in high-stress situations where you benefit most from meditation, such as a traffic jam, a stressful work meeting, or a long line at the grocery store.

- Convenient position. If you are seated, lying down, walking, or in other positions or activities, you should practice meditation. Try to be relaxed enough to get the most out of your meditation. Seek to maintain a healthy posture during meditation.

- Transparent heart. Without judgment, let the thoughts flow through your mind.

Practicing meditation daily

Don't let the idea of the "right" way of meditating add to your tension. You may attend special centers of meditation or community classes taught by qualified teachers if you want to. But you can easily practice meditation on your own, too.

And you can do the meditation as formal or casual as you want, but ensure it does match your lifestyle and circumstance. Some people integrate meditation into their everyday routines. They can begin and end each day, for example, with an hour of meditation. But what you need for meditation is a few minutes of quality time.

Here are several ways you can practice your meditation, whenever you want to:

- Deep breath. For beginners, this technique is fine, since breathing is a natural feature. Focus your whole concentration on breathing. Concentrate on feeling and listening as you breathe in and exhale through your nostrils. To breathe slowly and deeply. Kindly return your concentration to your breathing when your mind wanderers.

- Body scan. Shift attention to various parts of the body when using the technique. Be mindful of the different sensations in your body, whether this is pain, discomfort, warmth, or relaxation. Combine body scanning with breathing exercises and visualize various areas of your body breathing heat or relaxation.

- A mantra to repeat. You may make your motto,

religious or secular, as it may be. Examples of religious mantras include the Christian practice of Jesus Prayer, the holy name of God in Judaism, or the Hindu om chant, Buddhism, and other Eastern religions.

- Walking and meditating. The combination of a walk and meditation is an easy and safe way to relax. You can use this technique anywhere you walk, whether in a peaceful forest, on a town sidewalk, or in the market. When using this process, slow down your walking speed so you can concentrate on every step of your legs or feet. Don't concentrate on a specific destination. Concentrate on your legs and feet, repeating words of action in your mind such as 'lifting,' 'moving' and 'placing' as you raise each foot, move your leg forward, and put your foot on the ground.

- Pledge to prayer. Prayer is the best-known form of meditation and the most commonly performed. In most rituals of faith, spoken and written prayers find themselves. You may pray with words of your own, or read prayers written by others. Check your local bookstore's Self-Help section, for example. Speak about possible resources with your rabbi, priest, minister, or any other spiritual leader.

- Read and reflect. Many people report enjoying reading poetry or sacred texts and taking a few moments to focus quietly on their significance. You can also listen to sacred music, the words spoken, or any music that you find relaxing or inspiring. You might want to write your thoughts in a journal or talk to a friend or spiritual leader about them.

- Focus on caring and gratitude. In this form of meditation, you concentrate your focus on a holy image or being, weaving in your thoughts, feelings of devotion, compassion, and gratitude. You may also close your eyes, using your imagination, or look at image representations.

12 SCIENTIFIC BENEFITS OF MEDITATION

Meditation's popularity is growing, with more people

discovering its benefits.

Meditation is a repetitive process of training the mind to concentrate your thoughts and redirect them.

You can use it to raise awareness about yourself and the environment. Many people see it as a way of lowering stress and improving focus.

People can use the activity to develop other beneficial behaviors and emotions, such as good mood and attitude, self-discipline, healthier patterns of sleep, and even improved tolerance to pains.

Let's look at 12 benefits of meditation for the body.

1. Cuts back on the tension

One of the most common reasons people practice meditation is to reduce stress.

One research of more than 3,500 adults found that it lives up to its reputation for reducing stress.

Normally, increased levels of stress hormone cortisol are triggered by mental and physical stress. This causes many of the stress's harmful effects, like the release of inflammation-promoting chemicals called cytokines.

These effects can interfere with sleep, trigger depression and anxiety, increase blood pressure, and lead to tiredness and blurry thought.

In an eight-week study, a form of meditation called "meditation of mindfulness" decreased the response to inflammation caused by stress.

Another study of nearly 1,300 adults has shown that meditation can reduce stress. This impact was especially greatest in those with the highest stress levels.

Research has shown that meditation can also enhance stress-related symptoms, including irritable bowel syndrome, post-traumatic stress disorder, and fibromyalgia.

Many meditation types can help lower the tension. Meditation can also alleviate symptoms of people suffering from stress-induced medical conditions.

2. Control Anxiety

Moderate tension translates into less anxiety.

For example, an eight-week meditation study of mindfulness helped attendees minimize their anxiety.

It also decreased anxiety disorder symptoms such as phobias, social anxiety, negative thinking, obsessive-compulsive behaviors, and panic attacks.

Another research was followed up three years after 18 volunteers had completed an eight-week mediation program. Most participants had maintained daily therapy and held lower levels of long-term anxiety.

A larger study among 2,466 participants also found that several different mediation techniques would lower levels of anxiety.

Yoga has been shown, for example, to help people relieve anxiety. This is possibly due to benefits from both the practice of meditation and physical activity.

Meditation in high-pressure work environments can also help reduce job-related anxiety. One research showed a mediation program in a group of nurses has decreased anxiety.

Habitual therapy tends to relieve anxiety and mental health-related problems such as social anxiety, phobias, and obsessive-compulsive behaviors.

3. Promotes emotional wellbeing

Some types of meditation can also lead to a better self-image and a better perspective on life.

Two meditation carefulness research showed depression decreased in more than 4,600 adults.

One research accompanied 18 participants as they had spent three years practicing meditation. The study found that there were long-term decreases in depression among participants.

Inflammatory chemicals called cytokines, released in response to stress, may affect mood, leading to depression. An analysis of several studies indicates that by decreasing these inflammatory chemicals, meditation can alleviate depression.

Another controlled research compared electrical activity between the brains of people who practiced meditation for consciousness and those of those who did not.

Those who meditated showed significant improvements in behavior in positive thought and motivation related areas.

Certain types of meditation can boost depression and

establish a more optimistic life outlook. Research indicates that cultivating an ongoing meditation practice will help you to retain certain benefits in the long run.

4. Improves self-confidence

Some types of meditation can help you develop a better self-understanding, allowing you to evolve to your best self.

For example, a meditation on self-inquiry is specifically intended to help you gain a deeper understanding of yourself and how you relate to those around you.

Other types help you to recognize feelings that may be negative or losing yourself. The theory is that, as you become more aware of your thinking habits, you will guide them towards more positive trends.

A study of 21 women battling breast cancer showed that their self-esteem increased more than it did in those who attended social support sessions when they participated in a tai chi program.

In another report, 40 senior men and women taking a meditation awareness program reported reduced feelings of isolation relative to a control group put on the program's waiting list.

More imaginative problem solving can also be developed by practice in meditation.

Self-inquiry and similar meditation methods will allow you to "know yourself," which can be a starting point for other positive improvements.

5. Lengthens Attention Span

Focused-attention meditation is like elevating your attention span by weight. This helps to improve the attention's power and stamina.

For example, a study investigated the impact of an eight-week meditation course on mindfulness and found it enhanced the ability of participants to reorient and retain their focus.

A related study found that staff with human resources who frequently practiced meditation on mindfulness remained focused on a mission for longer.

These staff often recalled their duties in more detail than their colleagues who didn't practice meditation.

Also, one study concluded that meditation could also reverse brain patterns that lead to mind-walking, worrying, and poor focus.

You can also benefit from meditating for a short time. One study found four days of meditation practice that could be necessary to improve attention span.

Miscellaneous meditation styles will develop your ability to focus and sustain attention. This can have an impact with as little as four days of meditation.

6. Can reduce memory loss related to age

Improvements in mindfulness and clarity of thought can help keep your mind young.

Kirtan Kriya is a meditation method that combines a mantra or chant with repetitive finger movement to focus thoughts. It enhanced the capacity of participants to perform memory tasks in several studies of memory loss related to aging.

Also, a study of 12 studies showed that, in older participants, multiple meditation styles improved focus, memory, and mental pace.

In addition to combating normal age-related memory

loss, meditation in patients with dementia can at least partially improve memory. It may also help to reduce stress and improve coping for those caring for dementia family members.

The improved concentration that you can gain through daily meditation can enhance memory and clarity of mind. These benefits can help to prevent memory loss and dementia associated with aging.

7. Can Offer kindness

Especially certain forms of meditation can increase positive feelings and behavior towards yourself and others.

Metta, a form of meditation, also known as a meditation on love-kindness, starts to develop kind thoughts and feelings towards yourself.

Via practice, people learn to express this compassion and acceptance outwardly, first to relatives, then to acquaintances and eventually enemies.

Twenty-two studies of this method of meditation have shown its capacity to increase the compassion of peoples towards themselves and others.

One analysis of 100 adults randomly allocated to a program that included a meditation on loving-kindness found such benefits to be dose-dependent.

In other words, the more effort people put into a meditation on Metta, the more they had positive feelings.

Another group of studies showed the positive feelings that people build through Metta meditation could increase social anxiety, decrease marriage conflict, and help control anger.

These benefits often tend to accumulate over time through the practice of meditation on love-kindness.

Metta, or meditation on love-kindness, is a method of cultivating positive emotions, first for oneself and then for others. Metta increases positivity for others, empathy, and caring behavior.

8. May help combat addictions

By increasing your self-control and awareness of triggers for addictive behaviors, the mental discipline you can develop through meditation may help you break dependencies.

Research has shown that meditation can help people learn to focus their attention, increase their resilience, control their emotions and desires, and improve their understanding of the causes behind their addictive behaviors.

One research that taught 19 alcoholics how to meditate found that participants who received the training we're getting better at controlling their cravings and stress related to cravings.

Meditation can also help you manage your food cravings. A review of 14 studies found the meditation on mindfulness helped participants to reduce emotional and binge eating.

Meditation develops mental discipline and willpower and may help you avoid unwanted impulses triggers. This can help you recover, lose weight, and redirect other undesirable habits.

9. Improves sleep

At some point, nearly half the population will be struggling with insomnia.

One study compared two meditation programs based

on mindfulness by randomly assigning participants to one of two groups. One group had been practicing meditation, while the other did not.

Participants who meditated fell asleep earlier than those who did not meditate and stayed asleep longer.

Becoming skilled in meditation can help you control or redirect the thoughts of racing or "runaway," which often lead to insomnia.

It can also help relax your body, release tension, and put you in a peaceful state where you're more likely to fall asleep.

A variety of meditation techniques can help you relax and control the "runaway" thoughts, which may interfere with sleep. This may shorten the amount of time it takes to fall asleep and improve the quality of sleep.

10. Helps relieve pain

Your perception of pain is related to your state of mind, and in stressful conditions, it can be heightened.

For example, one study used functional MRI techniques to analyze brain activity when participants encountered a painful stimulus. Some participants had completed four days of meditation carefulness training, and others had not.

Patients who were meditating displayed increased activity in the brain centers known to control pain. Also, they registered less pain sensitivity.

In 3,500 participants, a broader study looked at the impact of repetitive meditation. It found that meditation was associated with reduced chronic or sporadic pain complaints.

Additional meditation research in patients with terminal meditation discovered can help to mitigate chronic end-of-life pain.

Meditators and non-meditators faced the same causes of pain in both of these cases. Still, meditators demonstrated a better capacity to deal with pain and also faced a decreased pain sensation.

Meditation will lessen the brain's perception of pain. This can benefit when used as an alternative to medical care or physical therapy to treat chronic pain.

11. Can reduce blood pressure

Meditation, too, can improve physical health by reducing heart pressure.

Over time, high blood pressure makes it harder for the heart to pump blood, which can result in impaired heart function.

High blood pressure also leads to atherosclerosis, or artery narrowing, which can cause heart attacks and strokes.

A study of 996 volunteers found that meditating on a "silent mantra" — a repetitive, non-vocalized phrase — reduced blood pressure on average by around five points.

This was more common among older volunteers and those who had pre-study higher blood pressure.

A review concluded that several types of meditation produced similar blood pressure changes.

In part, meditation helps to control blood pressure by calming the nerve signals that guide heart function, blood vessel tension, and the "fight-or-flight" response that increases alertness in stressful situations.

In individuals who meditate regularly, blood

pressure drops not only during meditation but also over time. This can lower the stress on the heart and arteries and help prevent heart disease.

12. Anywhere you can meditate

People practice several different meditation styles, most of which require no specialized equipment or space. With just a few minutes of daily work.

If you want to begin meditation, try choosing a meditation form based on what you want to get out of it.

CHAPTER 4

THE BEST RELATIONSHIP GOALS TO NURTURE INTIMACY

What are the relationship goals for couples?

The short answer is — the goals of the partnership are the hopes, aspirations, and accomplishments you and your partner or spouse create for the life you want to develop together.

You have your career goals or your personal life. You can have your own growth goals and self-improvement goals.

Just as we have personal or professional ambitions, partners should carefully consider a list of goals for the partnership and how to achieve them.

Over time, individuals and couples adjust, and these changes can lead to disconnection, tension, and unhappiness.

If you don't take the time to envision your perfect future as a couple, and how together you can develop and evolve, you will only develop apart.

But when the two of you work together towards a shared vision, while being flexible and agile when life changes occur, you will secure your relationship and enjoy all the benefits of having those objectives.

1: Make each Other a priority

Let's be frank — most of us talk about the meaning of our marriage or love relationship in a big game, but when the rubber hits the floor, we don't put each other first.

Over time, you're beginning to take each other for granted.

You get busy and overwhelmed with your things and forget to respond to your partner's needs and desires.

You see your coupling as a given, which is just a by-product of your relationship with this other person.

But the pairing is a different entity. There you are. Your partner's in there. And friendship is there.

You will have to accept yourself as the centerpiece of your life. How can you get this done?

- It is a responsibility you have to uphold with all your decisions and acts every single day.

- It involves regular recalibration, depending on each other's needs and what happens in your life.

Take a moment every day to ask each other and yourself, "Are we putting one another first today? What do we need to do to feed it today?"

2: Building a Bubble Pair

A couple of bubbles reinforce the goal of making your relationship a priority by speaking in terms of "us" rather than "me."

For most couples, this is hard because it involves first seeing yourself as part of a team, above your desires and behaviors.

But instead of weakening you through this interdependence, it strengthens you because everyone feels protected and loved.

Creating the aim of this couple takes a bit of time and commitment, but the payoff is massive as you create a safe sphere around your partnership.

The first step towards achieving this aim is to come together and make a set of agreements that will improve your relationship care and security.

One example of this might be "I would never deliberately scare you or abandon you," or "I would treat your vulnerabilities with respect and caution."

Also, a couple of bubble target includes:

- To become knowledgeable regarding the wants, expectations, and fears of one another.

- Fast repair of damage to the partnership.

- Build up a bank of good memories to offset any suffering.

- Being a pillar to each other in tough times.

3: Provide Daytime Connection

Spending one-on-one time together to reconnect is an important everyday objective of your relationship.

If one or both of you work outside the home, carving this time without disruptions or interruptions (from children or something else) is particularly crucial.

Try to do this both in the morning before the

beginning of the workday and in the evening before you're dragged away to the tasks and obligations.

The most important aspect of this period of a relationship is for you to be truly present for each other. This means you don't look at your computer, do a job or watch TV. You concentrate solely on one another.

This isn't the time to resolve your problems or work through conflict. It's a time to chat, connect, welcome, and just enjoy the company of one another.

Look into the eyes of each other. Keep your hands up. Attentively listen as the other talks.

In the morning, before you get up or over a cup of coffee, you could spend some time chatting in bed. You could go for a walk together in the evening or send the kids out to play while you relax and catch up on your day.

The link-time doesn't have to be long hours. Perhaps 15 or 20 minutes is enough to affirm how much you care for one another.

4: Communicate with Kindness

Goal-setting couples must include the ways you

interact with one another. But have you ever noticed how couples could talk so cruelly and unkindly to each other?

They tell one another things they would never dream of asking a casual acquaintance or even someone they don't like.

It's so quick to lash out and say hurtful things when we feel hurt, angry, or frustrated. Sometimes we use passive-aggressive terms and actions to communicate how we feel, using subtle digs, intimidation, or stonewalling.

Both direct and implicit words and actions like these are deeply wounding, accumulating enough over time to cause serious problems in a relationship. You lose confidence, mutual respect, and ultimately love.

Make it a priority in all your interactions to be kind. Being kind does not mean agreeing with each other or even feeling loved during a difficult moment.

It does mean that you consent not to strike, threaten, or purposely injure each other. It means speaking honestly without using passive or aggressive behavior.

It means that when you feel like lashing out, you step away or count to ten, knowing you don't want to say or do something you'll regret later.

We are all human, and there will, of course, be moments when you fall short of your target of kindness. But make it a priority to immediately apologize, offer immediate forgiveness, and reset your target of kindness as soon as possible.

5: Acknowledge vulnerability

Partner enters into a relationship with past baggage, insecurities, ashamed or guilty feelings, and tenuous hopes and dreams. We have vulnerabilities that we want to mask from others so that they don't think less about us.

As confidence and trust develop with each other, you share with your partner some of your flaws and inner pain.

You show your vulnerable underbelly in hopes of finding a position of comfort where you can truly be yourself.

Nothing is more wounding to the couple than

disregarding, or worse, rubbing your flaws back into your face to make you feel worse about yourself.

The freedom to be comfortably vulnerable to each other will reinforce the bond between you and cultivate a love and intimacy that is deeper than you thought possible.

When your partner accepts and treats your flaws with dignity, it can heal past wounds and make you feel more confident about who you are.

Make it a priority for one another to be transparent, truthful, and genuine. But most importantly, make it a priority to always treat one another's vulnerabilities with tender loving care.

6: The Fun Together Strategy

Life is already intense and stressed. You spend your days working, caring for kids, running errands, dealing with problems, and thinking about future issues.

Your relationship should be a place of peace and respite from the everyday tribulations. Your relationship should genuinely provide an outlet for the fullest possible enjoyment of life.

Think back to when you first met your love partner or spouse, and how much fun you had together.

You hadn't had to work too hard to have fun at that early stage of your relationship. Everything was fun, and you've been delighted to find fun things to do together.

When your closeness has grown, you may need to work a little harder together to build fun times, but that's still possible.

Make it a priority of scheduling and playing time every week. Sit down with your partner to chat about what you both perceive as fun activities. Be open to trying out new things that could be different from your initial fun ideas.

Let yourself be dumb and act like children again. Even brief, spontaneous moments of fun will deepen and bring you closer to your relationship.

7: Grasp the languages of your love

Gary Chapman outlines five ways people show themselves and feel love. Including:

- Giving-gifts

- Calendar time

- Words of affirmation

- Actions of service

- Body touch

Chapman argues that each of us has a primary and secondary love language that is reflected in the way we show love to others.

But we're exposing our deepest needs within the relationship by expressing our love language to our partner.

If you're extremely affectionate with your partner, for example, it shows you're looking for physical affection from him or her.

Each of you may not have the same love language, and that's why it's so important that you both learn and respect each other's love language.

You can do that by studying how your partner expresses love to you and by examining what he or she talks about within the relationship.

Another way of learning about your love languages is by taking a love language quiz and sharing the results.

Once you are both conscious of each other's love language, your goal is to offer your partner more of what he or she needs in the relationship.

8: Hold a Satisfying Sex Life

No matter how great your sex life was at the start of your relationship, it's inevitable from time to time that it will grow boring or even burdensome.

If you're fifteen or twenty years into a marriage, it can take real effort and commitment to maintain that romantic spark. But for a healthy relationship, healthy sex life is crucial.

Maintaining a satisfactory sexual bond involves understanding your partner and their sex-related needs, as well as speaking up for their own needs.

Women need to feel comfortable and secure with their partner to be willing to try new things and be sexually adventurous.

Men need more variety and visual stimulation than females do.

Sex can become a stressor for women if they see it as yet another chore they must perform.

Men see sex as a stress reliever and need to experience closeness to this physical connection.

Regular communication is the key to bridging those differences in sexual needs.

Speaking about your sex life may at first feel uncomfortable, but communicating your needs and concerns will protect your relationship from potential problems that could further damage your intimacy.

Make it a target for a weekly discussion of your sex life. Be frank with each other about what you want, what does not fit well, and what you're fantasizing about.

Work to make your relationship feel secure, comfortable, and connected and try to negotiate a compromise in different needs areas.

9: Promoting One Other Goal

As important as creating a couple of bubbles in your relationship is, you are two individuals who have their own goals and dreams. Having your own goals and dreams as a person does not weaken your bond.

On the opposite, as each partner has something unique and interesting to add to the partnership, it should strengthen the relationship.

You both should feel that the most important person in your life — your spouse or partner — will help and respect your ambitions and celebrate your accomplishments.

Supporting each other's interests is more than merely offering support or verbal encouragement. It could mean sacrificing time, money, or obligations to prove you are fully on board.

Make it a priority to explore your individual goals and dreams, and how you can achieve those goals together.

Ask each other questions such as, "What can I do to help your targets?

10: Have a Yearly Review

If you and your partner take the time to set goals for a relationship and work towards achieving them, then measuring the success of your efforts is significant.

Sit down together at the end of the year to address

each of the priorities you've established for your partnership.

- What have you done to realize those goals in the past year?

- So how good were you?

- What does it take you to continue working on?

Use this time to set new goals for the coming year, building on what you've done and what you've learned from each other in the past year.

11: Spice Up The Date Nights

If you balked at goal #8 with the word "maintain," then it's time to put the spice back into your one-on-one time. And if that doesn't suffice, now is the time to make it a priority.

It's not just about getting the kids on well. That's not going to be enough to hold your marriage bond strong. And whether you admit it or not, you will both be miserable if you give each other a quick, goodnight peck on the lips, the closest you get to the intimacy.

So schedule a regular date night with that

commitment and let nothing but a real emergency mess. And if you're not sure what to do to reconnect and pave the path to greater intimacy, it can't hurt brainstorming ideas and making it fun together.

What can you do this week to remember the fun times you had when you first began dating yourself and your spouse? Which date will make you closer than you've been for a while?

Your spouse may still be in the dark about what's turning you on, but you're probably not.

The best time to share that information without putting pressure on your spouse is during these private dates — whether you're chatting in your bedroom together with or talking about a drink at a favorite restaurant.

The more you can make your partner feel special and worth some trouble at least, the more likely you're both to make inroads and start building a connection — or repairing it.

And with that in place, it's not hard to get a fire going if you're both open to greater intimacy. Then you can do the work to keep it.

12: Build a Diary for the Couple

Get a journal and write your partner a letter in it, share your thoughts and worries, and express your expectations for your relationship.

- Write down what you love about your partner and what you would love to do as a couple.

- Write down how much fun you have had and what you think you can still do as you grow older.

- Let your spouse read your submission and write your own.

You can even participate in some quizzes about relationships and share your answers in your blog.

Journaling as a couple will start as part of the counseling for couples and become a regular part of the therapy for your DIY couple.

Keeping a journal together and making it a safe place to be honest about what you think and feel can draw both of you closer together and help each other work through personal challenges.

There is sound science behind the benefits of journaling for the mental health of an individual. When two are involved — especially two who are committed to the well-being of each other — the combined benefits can only help to strengthen their relationship.

GOALS FOR LONG TERM RELATIONSHIP

Your marriage or engaged relationship will develop and evolve— and you want your love and closeness to stand the test of time.

As the years go by, you and your partner can grow and have different needs, and if you have expectations for shared and actual relationships, you've created a shield against obstacles that often tear couples apart.

Setting goals for couples encourage both of you to set the bar high for your relationship as opposed to allowing your connection to wilt and erode.

A life-long pursuit should be to have expectations for your relationship — one that takes you together and enhances your love year after year. Here are some long-term goals for the relationship:

13: Schedule Travel Together

Was there a spot for your honeymoon that you both wanted to go but couldn't afford? Or is there another, more accessible paradise that suits both of you?

Range it out with your partner and spend the daydreaming time together to make sure you both have a great time.

Couples worldwide can attest to the advantages of traveling together. And those trips can be planned together to strengthen your bond and increase intimacy.

How short or long you've got for a couple of holidays or annual vacation, it's always better if you're both involved in planning the specifics that will most affect you both:

- Wherever you go, and where you want to see the sites

- Where to rest

- How much travel budget you should spend

- How long should travel be

- Whether you want to fly with others, or not

Don't assume you know what your partner wants, because even if you already knew what he or she might want to change for the next holiday.

14: Planning Dates schedule

The science behind planning your goals as a couple reinforces the idea many couples learned on their own: it can be fun to plan together.

It is not just about retirement planning, either. Together you can set goals to...

- Your friendship with them

- Parenting / your kids

- Their professions and their interests

- Your fitness and physical and mental health

- Financial stability

It couldn't sound like the most romantic way of being together. But if you actively involve your partner together in preparing for a better future, this can be very romantic indeed.

Together preparation is a powerful way of strengthening the relationship as a couple. So place a date on the calendar, make sure you have no interruptions, and spend a couple of hours on your annual review of the relationship.

15: schedule weekly Health Marriage meetings

The best piece of advice that you can get is to discuss your connection's health regularly. It's beneficial to schedule "meetings," along with preparation, to monitor the progress and make any appropriate changes to the plan.

It's also a good way to get to grips with how you do it, and whether you can all work together as a team.

Set a weekly "planning date" to review the progress of the previous week, draw up a to-do list for the next week, and address any relevant issues.

Play the Truth Game if there's a sticky topic that keeps coming up — and one of you likes to chat five or ten times more than the other —

- Take turns to ask the other about a deep personal concern.

- Do not automatically respond to your question with your take on it after the other person answers it; instead, let the other person ask his or her question.

- The next issue shouldn't be linked to the previous one.

- Respond as truthfully as you can to this issue.

- Repeat, if the time is up for more.

If you feel the need to answer one of the answers provided by your spouse, ask before you launch into it. He or she might not be up for an extended conversation, much less debate, depending on the time of day and the sort of day you have both had.

Even if you can see it from other viewpoints for both of you, sometimes you just don't have the resources. Accept that and live to speak a different day.

16: Use Stimuli to improve Romance

This may be a sequence of if-then sentences, such as:

If my wife has trouble finding clothes that make her feel comfortable, then I will do something or say something to remind her that she looks amazing to me no matter what she wears.

It's not just a matter of expressing your interest in intimacy, because you could just see her as your only sexual partner for all she knows.

Let those random acts be about persuading your partner that she (or he) still makes your stomach flip (or your heart flips) and that she is still the only woman on earth who can do that.

Try one of the causes, then:

- If my spouse sighs or makes some other noise that shows discomfort or dissatisfaction with his presence, then I'll say something like, "Those pants look phenomenal on you."

- If we eat out and I think my spouse may be nervous about ordering what he or she wants, then I'm going to suggest something like, "Let's just order exactly what we want and savor every bite. No peeking at the nutrition detail. You do not have to think about something."

- If I see flowers dying in our house, I'll buy another bouquet while I'm out and put a note of love in it for him/her.

17: Give Gifts for Fun

These needn't be costly, and — especially if you save money together. It's best to stick to cheap presents, consumable or otherwise, just to show your partner that you're still very keen to keep the romance alive.

Here are some suggestions:

- Borrow films from the library you are both interested in.

- Lend music CDs to party together.

- Take a bouquet of colorful flowers or balloons.

- If your partner is involved or has a hobby, pick up something relevant to that.

- Delight your partner by offering a single treatment that he or she loves.

Especially if the gift-giving language of your partner's love, this is a powerful way to keep the romance alive. Suppose you keep the tank full of affection, so intimacy is much more possible.

18: Carrying out routine thoughtful acts

If the love language of your partner is service actions,

spontaneous or routine thoughtfulness acts will enhance how much you care.

It tells your partner that you have paid attention and that you are always motivated to help out and be there for him or her.

Consider the possibilities of:

- Upon seeing a garbage container complete, clean it, and replace the cover.

- If you find that your partner is distracted with something, offer to do an errand, pick up someone, etc.

- If you've cooked dinner with your partner, try to clean up — or assist with laundry.

- When your wife is tired, give a massage, a cup of tea, a hot bath, and so on.

- If your partner seems to be on edge, ask if you could do something to make the day easier.

Only displaying your readiness to help can go a long way to telling your partner that their health and well-being are vital to you

19: Seeking common ground

Both of you have your interests, but taking a class together at least once a year (if not more often) is a perfect way to grow a common interest and discover a new way to have fun.

You might learn something that can save a life, too.

Find out the possibilities here:

- Cooking or baking

- Dance (waltz, tango, salsa, etc.)

- Learning a Language

- Self-defense or martial arts

- Learning to play an instrument

- Compounding

- Vehicle repair

- CPR and First Aid

You may take one class a year and then arrange opportunities to practice what you have learned. Or you could take two classes a year — one in late winter or early spring, and the other one in late summer or early fall.

Be sure to consult with your partner and make sure you are both sincerely interested in attending before you pay for the class.

20: Have a Picnic each month

Possibly you've got your favorite spots, or you might try something new. The important thing is to spend time together, to savor the meal and the company of each other.

You could go for a romantic picnic in your backyard, in a park, on the beach, or the floor of your apartment.

If you do this at home, and you have children, make sure they don't disturb you unless someone dies or the house is on fire.

You can also plan a horse-drawn carriage ride to the park or the beach or lakeshore where you will have your picnic-either on the sand or a ferry.

Do what you can for any date to mix it up. If both of you agree to this, organizing your monthly picnic will take turns, and it can be as simple or elaborate as you want.

21: Go to Cinema Weekly

Take turns choosing a film each month and go out to watch it together. You can either come out for dinner or dessert (or both) or head home after the movie.

It doesn't matter if the film wasn't an Academy Award winner itself. What counts is how much fun you have while, and afterward, you are there.

You can also choose a drive-in movie theater, enjoy your take-out picnic, and switch to the back seat if more action is taking place in the car than on the screen.

If you can't manage this every month, try at least every quarter to do that or something similar.

Just spend some time together, watching something that reminds you for as long as you can of what you have together and what you want to have together.

22: Send Love Notes

You may write these on different pieces of paper (or cardstock) or in the journal of a pair, in which you take turns to write.

You should pin up the latest love notes on a bulletin

board to keep it open, that you can't help but see every day.

Pin it lose or position it in an envelope that has an image of the recipient of the letter.

When replacing your letter with a new note, flip the envelope to show the words "You have mail! "Or" Thinking about you" or something else that will get the attention of your spouse.

Don't be disappointed if it doesn't open up immediately. If your partner knows how the letters work, it's just a matter of time before your new love note is read.

Use them not to sell but to remind your partner of something that you love about him or her — and perhaps something that you want to do together.

Keep it positive, supportive, and caring. Let they intend to remember what you have to each other and to celebrate the progress you have made — together and individually.

23: Give your partner a break from the children

If you can both handle it, you can make this a

monthly or quarterly thing. Or one of you might grab a moment when the other needs a break and offer to take the children on vacation.

Of course, if your partner responds with "No, don't leave me," you may need to reconsider your strategy and find a babysitter while you are performing a much-needed joint TLC procedure.

It is important to spend time together as a family, but that family's credibility depends on the link between you and your spouse. And when things get bad, it's not enough just to do damage control. Creating the relation and maintaining it must be a regular priority.

If we want to make sure we're doing something that our happiness — and that of those closest to us — depends on, we're not trying to squeeze it into; we're making time for it. And that is what we intend for.

If other things get in the way, then we do what's needed to restore order and bring peace to the land (i.e., homefront).

So, take the kids out and give them time to chill your spouse — or have the kids chill while you and your spouse tend to each other.

Do what's required and put your relationship ahead of what people want from you, besides your partner. You will both be proud to have done so.

CHAPTER 5
CONCLUSION

In conclusion, not just one thing helps a good relationship, but several things support it. A good relationship where two or more people are related through something, whether it is blood, marriage, or mutual affection, requires a steady dose of contact, similar goals, respect, and trust – the four pillars for any effective connection.

When it comes to people-to-people relationships, the trick is to optimize those moments of selflessness and concentrate on that other person or group. This particularly applies to those who have family members and spouses-or would-be spouses. But without the other three pillars, these relationships would also fall to the ground – without trust and respect, and commonalities shared and practiced among the people comprising these relationships.

Relationships once again require constant work and focus and persistence-but it should be worth it: good, happy, and healthy relationships are equal to a high quality of life. Research indicates that to live long, happy and healthy lives, people need other people, which needs happy and healthy relations between people. It is, really, a simple notion. But it works-and it has always been working.

To fall in love is supposed to be magical, but to get close to another person is not at the best of times without there being highs and lows. Intimacy is a medium for every possible emotion, from the joy of learning that someone pretty wonderful is as moved by you as you are by them, to the anguish of self-doubt and possible loss, to the comfort, richness and sometimes stillness of a deeper love. Anxiety affects relationships, but you can secure your relationship and make it one that is solid, close and resilient by being open to its effect and actively reacting to it.

CPSIA information can be obtained
at www.ICGtesting.com
Printed in the USA
LVHW050800120221
679113LV00017B/600